Searchlight BOOKS™

What Do You Know about Maps?

Using

Economic and Resource Maps

Tracy Nelson Maurer

Lerner Publications • Minneapolis

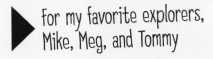

For my favorite explorers,
Mike, Meg, and Tommy

Cover image: This map shows a key natural and economic resource from each one of the fifty US states as of 2015, according to the United States Department of Agriculture Economic Research Service. The product shown for each state is one of that state's top five agricultural commodities. No data is available for the District of Columbia.

Lerner Publications Company
A division of Lerner Publishing Group, Inc.
241 First Avenue North
Minneapolis, MN 55401 USA

For reading levels and more information, look up this title
at www.lernerbooks.com.

Library of Congress Cataloging-in-Publication Data

Names: Maurer, Tracy, 1965– author.
Title: Using economic and resource maps / Tracy Nelson Maurer.
Description: Minneapolis : Lerner Publications, 2016. | Series: Searchlight books what do
    you know about maps? | Includes bibliographical references and index.
Identifiers: LCCN 2015038781| ISBN 9781512409512 (lb : alk. paper) | ISBN
    9781512412925 (pb : alk. paper) | ISBN 9781512410716 (eb pdf)
Subjects: LCSH: Map reading—Juvenile literature. | Economic geography—Maps—
    Juvenile literature. | Natural resources—Maps—Juvenile literature.
Classification: LCC GA130 .M44 2016 | DDC 912.01/4—dc23

LC record available at http://lccn.loc.gov/2015038781

Manufactured in the United States of America
1 – VP – 7/15/16

Contents

Chapter 1

WHAT ARE ECONOMIC AND RESOURCE MAPS?

Where are you? What cities or lakes are near you? What states or countries border your location? You can find the answers to all these questions by looking at a map!

This map shows roads and important places in Sacramento, California. What other information might be included on a map?

SACRAMENTO

Amtrak Station

3rd St
I St
J St
6th St
9th St
10th St
11th St
12th St
14th St

Plaza Mall

River

Tower Bridge

Crocker Park

Capitol Mall

K-St Mall

Governor's Mansion
State Historic Park

Sacramento Convention Center

Crocker Art Museum

State Capitol

Capitol Park

L St

21st St
23rd St

Roosevelt Park

N St

Sutter's Fort S Historical Pa

3rd St
5th St

Sacramento

Fremont Park

19th St

26th St

T St
U St
V St

South Side Park

11th St
13th St
15th St
16th St
18th St
22nd St

Wi Pa

Broadway

21st St

28th

0 —— 500 m
0 —— 500 yards

Maps use graphics to stand for different places. Maps also share information about the living or nonliving things you might find in those places. This information could include numbers showing how many people live in a state. Or it might be lines and labels showing roads in your city.

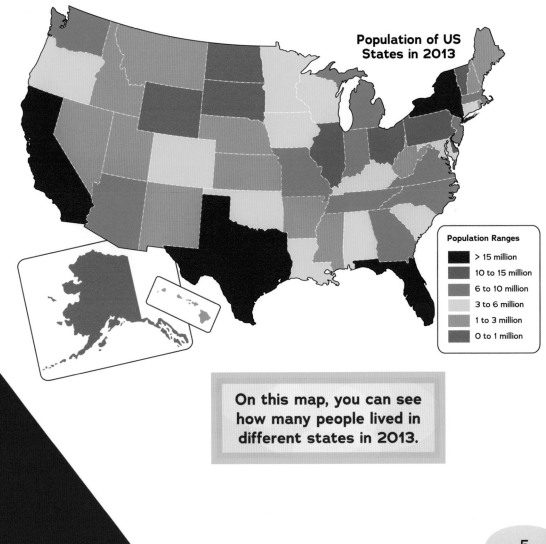

Population of US States in 2013

Population Ranges

- > 15 million
- 10 to 15 million
- 6 to 10 million
- 3 to 6 million
- 1 to 3 million
- 0 to 1 million

On this map, you can see how many people lived in different states in 2013.

People use maps for different reasons. Drivers might use a map that shows roads to keep from getting lost. A traveler may look at a map that shows countries to find out what nations border Kenya—the next place she plans to visit. A student writing a report on North Carolina would probably find it helpful to look at a map showing agricultural (farming) products from that state. A map like this would help the student report on what crops grow in North Carolina. Maps that show what crops or natural resources are in a place or how people in that place earn money are called economic and resource maps.

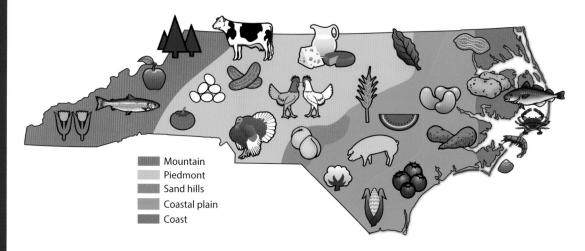

Mountain
Piedmont
Sand hills
Coastal plain
Coast

This map of North Carolina shows what agricultural products come from the state. Each picture stands for a different product.

The crops or resources a place has and how people earn money are often related. For example, if a resource map shows that a lake has lots of fish in it, then families may decide to travel there to fish. That brings tourism to the area. Tourism is the business of providing places to stay, food to eat, and hospitality to people who visit an area. People who visit a fishing area may rent a cabin there, eat at local restaurants, and hire a local fishing guide. This brings in tourism dollars.

Crappie/bluegill
Walleye/saugeye
Walleye trolling
Catfish
Largemouth bass
White bass
Road

Indian Lake

This is a map of fishing spots in Indian Lake, Ohio.

Early Resource Maps

No one knows for sure, but the first resource maps probably showed where to hunt. Can you guess why this was important for people to know? It's because their survival depended on knowing the location of animals they could hunt for food. Hunting was a common topic in early art as well. This shows that hunting mattered a great deal to many early peoples.

Hunting is the topic of this rock painting in Libya. Why is hunting such a common topic in early maps and art?

How Else Can Economic and Resource Maps Help?

Economic and resource maps can help you understand how a certain topic—say, farming—is connected to a certain place. They help you see what activities might be common in an area. They can also help you make a decision about a topic. If you want to pick apples at an orchard in your state, an economic and resource map can show you where in your state the most apples grow.

You wouldn't use an economic or resource map to find your way to Buffalo, New York. But if you want to learn what minerals are mined in China or where to find the state park nearest to your home, then reach for an economic or resource map!

This map shows state parks and recreation areas in Minnesota. Which ones might you visit if you lived in southeastern Minnesota? (Hint: The compass rose on the right shows which way is southeast.)

Chapter 2

WHAT'S ON ECONOMIC AND RESOURCE MAPS?

Cartographers are people who make maps. They try to put correct and current information on their maps. They use facts gathered by governments, universities, or research groups. Researchers count, measure, and sort data about everything and anything, from the number of trees in a city park to computer users around the world.

A cartographer works on a map in the early 1990s. What do cartographers do?

Census Data and Mapping

The United States Census Bureau is a main source of information for economic and resource maps. This agency counts the country's population using a survey called a census. The Census Bureau completes a full census every ten years and about two hundred smaller surveys each year.

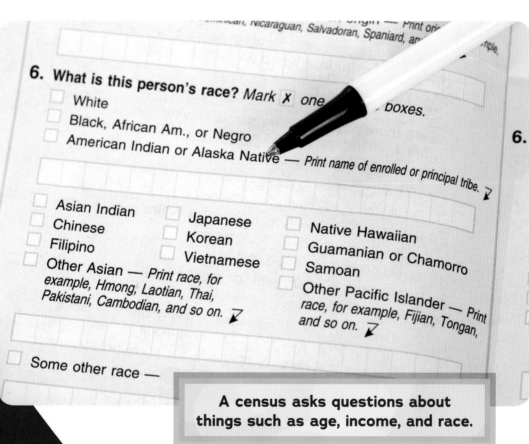

6. What is this person's race? Mark X one boxes.

☐ White
☐ Black, African Am., or Negro
☐ American Indian or Alaska Native — Print name of enrolled or principal tribe.

☐ Asian Indian ☐ Japanese ☐ Native Hawaiian
☐ Chinese ☐ Korean ☐ Guamanian or Chamorro
☐ Filipino ☐ Vietnamese ☐ Samoan
☐ Other Asian — Print race, for example, Hmong, Laotian, Thai, Pakistani, Cambodian, and so on. ☐ Other Pacific Islander — Print race, for example, Fijian, Tongan, and so on.

☐ Some other race —

A census asks questions about things such as age, income, and race.

Did You Know?

Population data may use the Latin term *per capita*. It means "by head," and it shows an average per person. For example, if the income in a country was $32,000 a year per capita, this means that, on average, each person in that country had an annual income of $32,000. Since this is an average, some people would have a lower income while others would have a higher income. What would it mean if you learned that Americans spent $703 per capita on holiday gifts in 2013?

Stores often keep track of per capita spending. It helps them plan things such as how many items to put on their shelves.

Researchers use computers to sort the survey facts collected by the Census Bureau. They plug the numbers into formulas and charts to make the data easier to understand.

So what types of census data might you see on an economic or resource map? Data about quantity, or the total count of something, is one type. For example, you might find information about the population of a particular state. Data about averages is another type. An economic map might highlight the average annual household income in certain cities, for instance.

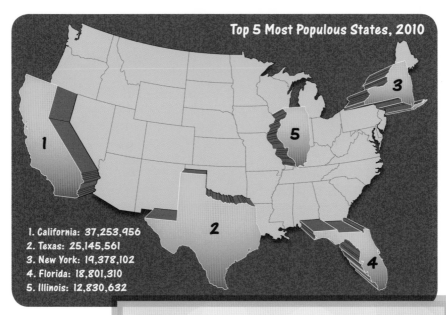

Top 5 Most Populous States, 2010

1. California: 37,253,956
2. Texas: 25,145,561
3. New York: 19,378,102
4. Florida: 18,801,310
5. Illinois: 12,830,632

This map shows the five states with the highest populations, according to the 2010 census. Is your state one of them?

Other types of data that might be on an economic or resource map are ratios and percentages. Ratio is the relationship in quantity, amount, or size between two or more things. For example, the ratio of computers to students in a school might be two to five. This means there are two computers for every five students. This ratio would be written as 2:5.

On this map, you can see the ratio of boys to girls in different states in India in 2011.

Boys per 100 Girls

- 125:130
- 115:120
- 111:115
- 107:111
- 103:107
- 101:103

Percentage is the count or portion of a whole. So say that out of the whole population in the United States, about 17 percent is Hispanic. On maps, that percentage might be written as 17%. Notice the percentage sign after the number.

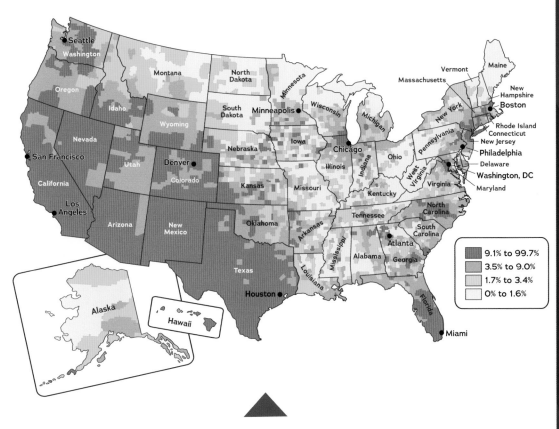

Legend:
- 9.1% to 99.7%
- 3.5% to 9.0%
- 1.7% to 3.4%
- 0% to 1.6%

THIS MAP LETS YOU SEE THE PERCENTAGE OF HISPANICS THAT LIVE IN DIFFERENT PARTS OF THE UNITED STATES.

Symbols and Colors

Mapmakers turn the data they get from the Census Bureau and other sources into symbols or colors. Not all maps use the same symbols to mean the same thing. Smokestack symbols may mean factories on one map. They might mean air pollution on another. Mapmakers use color in different ways too. Some mapmakers use many colors, while others use shades of just one color.

The maker of this map used corn symbols to show where in the United States the most corn is grown.

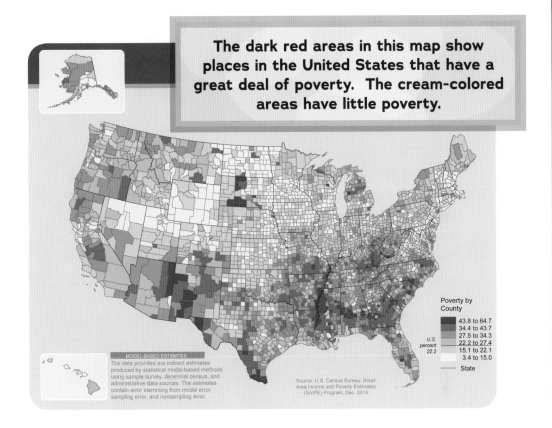

The dark red areas in this map show places in the United States that have a great deal of poverty. The cream-colored areas have little poverty.

Poverty by County

43.8 to 64.7
34.4 to 43.7
27.5 to 34.3
22.2 to 27.4
15.1 to 22.1
3.4 to 15.0

State

U.S. percent 22.2

MODEL-BASED ESTIMATES
The data provided are indirect estimates produced by statistical model-based methods using sample survey, decennial census, and administrative data sources. The estimates contain error stemming from model error, sampling error, and nonsampling error.

Source: U.S. Census Bureau, Small Area Income and Poverty Estimates (SAIPE) Program, Dec. 2014

Mapmakers also might include shaded colors or patterns on a map to show different amounts of something. A dark color may show that more of something is in a certain area, such as people of a certain age. A lighter color might mean there is less of something.

Dot Maps

Like color, dots can be a great tool for showing information on a map. Maps that use dots often show a quantity of something across a certain area. On a dot map, a dot might stand for one thing, such as one dot for one person. Or a dot might equal many things, such as one dot for ten thousand people. Each dot in a dot map shows a place where data was counted.

In this map from 2009, each dot stands for a public library. Can you point to three places that look as if they had many public libraries in 2009?

Scale

In addition to symbols and colors, mapmakers often put a scale on a map. A scale explains the size of a map compared to the place it represents. A mapmaker couldn't draw the United States at its actual size. The map would be enormous! Instead, mapmakers draw the country in a size that fits on a map. They then put a scale on the map to tell map users that, for example, 1 inch (2.54 centimeters) on their map equals 1,000 miles (1,609 kilometers). Scales are often near the bottom of a map.

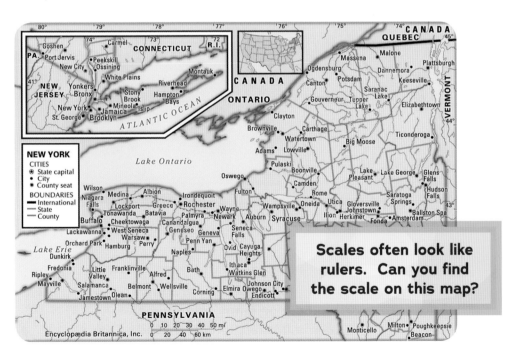

Scales often look like rulers. Can you find the scale on this map?

Keys

Keys, or legends, are another common feature on maps. Keys explain what a map's symbols or colors mean. Mapmakers often place the key in a box on the map. They sometimes state the map's theme or title in the key too. Some mapmakers also cite the source of their data in the key. For example, if they took population figures from the census of 2010, they might cite the Census Bureau as their source.

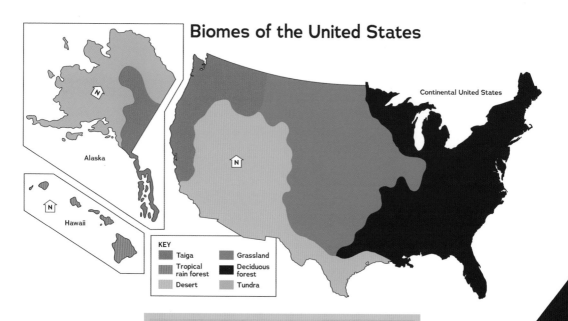

Biomes of the United States

Continental United States

Alaska

Hawaii

KEY
- Taiga
- Tropical rain forest
- Desert
- Grassland
- Deciduous forest
- Tundra

This map shows different biomes, or plant and animal communities, in the United States. What is the biome in the area where you live?

Chapter 3

HOW DO YOU USE ECONOMIC AND RESOURCE MAPS?

Using economic maps and resource maps means thinking about both a place and its connection to people, animals, plants, or nonliving things. These maps answer two questions at once: "Where is this location?" and "What facts do researchers know about living or nonliving things there?"

If you're wondering where the state of Virginia is, this map can help you find out. What does it tell you about how many people lived in Virginia in 2000?

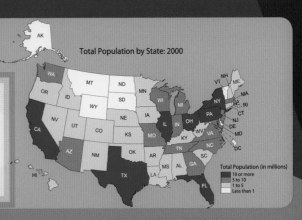

Total Population by State: 2000

Total Population (in millions)
- 10 or more
- 5 to 10
- 1 to 5
- Less than 1

Scientists, government leaders, teachers, reporters, health-care workers, and many other people use economic and resource maps. Economic maps often show causes or effects of poverty. Resource maps commonly show facts about rain forests, glaciers, energy use, global warming, and invasive species.

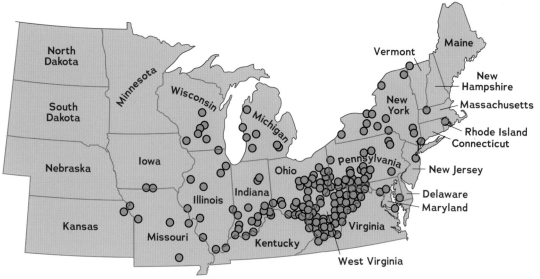

◉ Approximate locations of black locust

Black locust trees are an invasive species that mainly affects the northeastern United States. Look at this map to see which states these trees affect.

Economic maps can help you understand how people earn, save, or spend money. An economic map from a group called the World Bank shows where people live on less than $1.25 a day. Government leaders or charities might use this data to choose where to send aid.

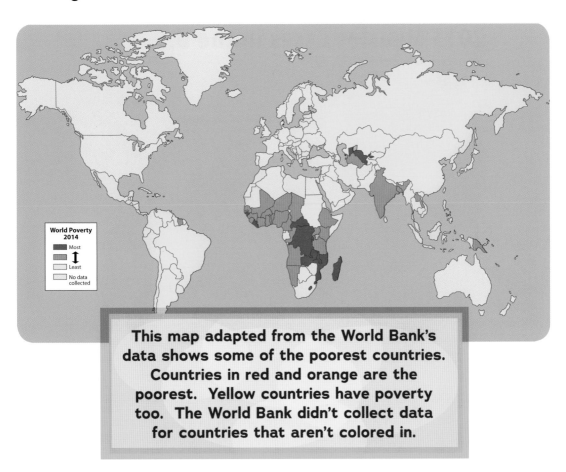

World Poverty
2014
Most
1
Least
No data
collected

This map adapted from the World Bank's data shows some of the poorest countries. Countries in red and orange are the poorest. Yellow countries have poverty too. The World Bank didn't collect data for countries that aren't colored in.

Resource maps can help doctors keep diseases from spreading. The Centers for Disease Control and Prevention provides maps for outbreaks of illnesses. Doctors look to these maps to see which countries need medical help and what shots people might need if they plan to visit those countries.

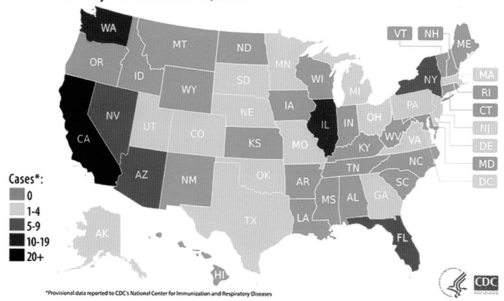

2015 Measles Cases in the U.S.
January 1 to November 13, 2015

Cases*:
- 0
- 1-4
- 5-9
- 10-19
- 20+

*Provisional data reported to CDC's National Center for Immunization and Respiratory Diseases

This map reveals which states were affected by measles within a certain time period.

Maps save lives! One of the earliest dot maps showed the location of cholera victims in 1854. Cholera is a very deadly disease. The information in the dot map revealed that sewers were close to water supplies, making people ill. Similar dot maps are still used to track diseases like malaria, avian flu, and Ebola.

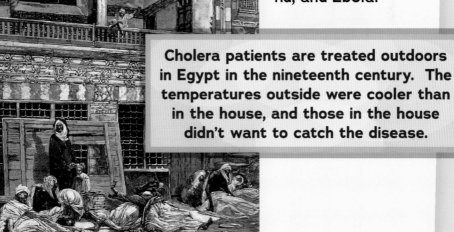

Cholera patients are treated outdoors in Egypt in the nineteenth century. The temperatures outside were cooler than in the house, and those in the house didn't want to catch the disease.

Economic Maps, Resource Maps, and You

In school, economic and resource maps can help you learn about places nearby or far away. These maps can build your understanding of a place.

You can find economic and resource maps in books and on the Internet. Entering keywords, such as "United States population maps," into your favorite search engine is a good place to start. Then look for maps from reliable websites, such as the Census Bureau and universities. Librarians can help you find books and databases that include reliable maps.

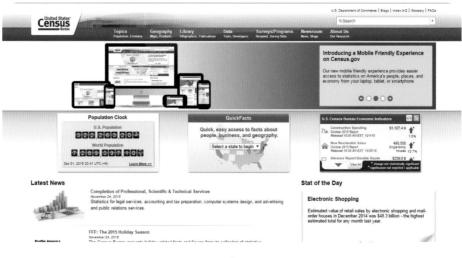

THE US CENSUS BUREAU'S WEBSITE IS AN EXCELLENT PLACE TO FIND RELIABLE MAPS.

Putting Economic and Resource Maps to the Test

Say you were writing a report about the continent of Africa. You might look at economic maps to understand where people need jobs. Resource maps can show you what materials come from the land to support industries that hire workers.

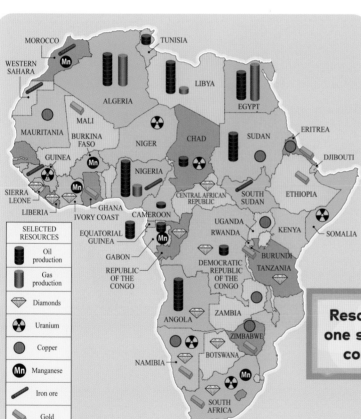

SELECTED RESOURCES

Oil production	
Gas production	
Diamonds	
Uranium	
Copper	
Manganese	Mn
Iron ore	
Gold	

Resource maps like this one show what materials come from the land.

You can also learn what life might be like for people in different parts of Africa. Look at the types of crops people in a certain area grow. You can look at the average rainfall for the area too. That's a natural resource that impacts crop harvests.

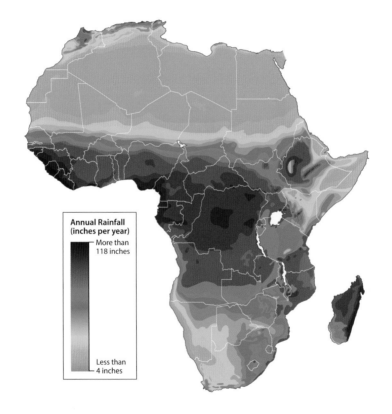

Annual Rainfall
(inches per year)

More than
118 inches

Less than
4 inches

A map about rainfall can help explain why people in an area grow the crops they do. Some crops need lots of rain, while others thrive in drier conditions.

Economic and resource maps can lead to deeper thinking about a place and what you find there. Does the location of a place and its natural resources change how people live there? How do people change a place?

THE LAND IN GREENLAND IS COLD AND SNOWY. HOW MIGHT THIS AFFECT THE LIVES OF THOSE WHO CALL IT HOME?

Sometimes economic and resource maps are most useful when you compare information from the past to the present. Mapmakers may show two maps from different times side by side. They could also show changes over time with graphics or lines.

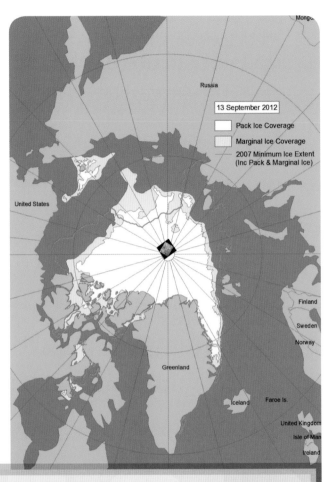

Russia

13 September 2012

Pack Ice Coverage

Marginal Ice Coverage

2007 Minimum Ice Extent
(Inc Pack & Marginal Ice)

United States

Finland

Sweden

Norway

Greenland

Iceland   Faroe Is.

United Kingdom

Isle of Man

Ireland

This map uses an orange line to show where ice used to be in a certain area in 2007. The white and gray colors show where ice was in 2012. You can see that some ice melted between 2007 and 2012.

Once you start looking, you'll see that maps are everywhere!

Economic maps and resource maps increase our knowledge of places, people, and things, and how they connect to one another. Watch for these maps online, in textbooks, or in news articles. You'll be surprised how often you see them!

Chapter 4

ARE YOU AN ECONOMIC AND RESOURCE MAP WHIZ?

Imagine you won a trip to any US location. Say your favorite thing to do is hike in the mountains. Use this map to pick three states you might visit.

Can you also find three states where you could fish?

Your friend wants to join you on your trip. He loves the outdoors as much as you do, but his favorite thing is forests. Is there a place you could go that has both mountains and trees? Look at the map on the facing page to find the answer.

Mountains and forests are both common attractions for travelers.

Things just got more complicated! Your grandmother also wants to travel with you. She would like to stay near water. What states do you think would make you, your friend, and your grandma happy?

MANY PEOPLE LIKE STAYING NEAR THE OCEAN.

Let's say you decided to visit Maine. It has mountains for you, trees for your friend, and water for your grandma. The trip will be a blast, but first, you have to do some homework. Your teacher has asked you to report on the economy of Maine before you leave for your trip. Look at the economic map below. Which industries employ the most people in Maine?

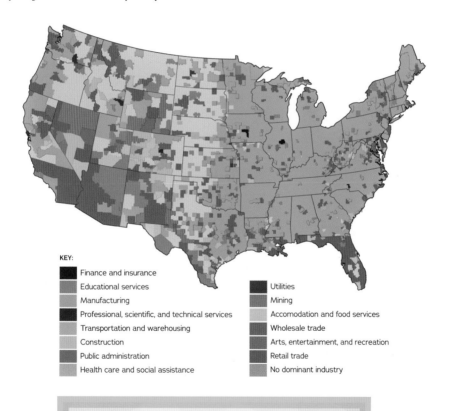

KEY:

■	Finance and insurance		
■	Educational services	■	Utilities
■	Manufacturing	■	Mining
■	Professional, scientific, and technical services	■	Accomodation and food services
■	Transportation and warehousing	■	Wholesale trade
■	Construction	■	Arts, entertainment, and recreation
■	Public administration	■	Retail trade
■	Health care and social assistance	■	No dominant industry

After you've named the biggest industries in Maine, can you find the major industries for your state?

Globes and maps are excellent learning tools.

You Did It!

Good work! You've just applied the knowledge that you learned. Economic and resource maps can teach you all kinds of things about all kinds of places in the world. Where would you like to learn about next?

Fun Facts

- Economic and resource maps are also called thematic maps. That's because they focus on one theme, or topic, connected to a location.

- In 2015, a huge earthquake struck Nepal. But thanks in part to online maps, rescuers were able to help. The maps showed instant updates to safe routes for reaching those in need.

- Rubber ducks have helped scientists understand ocean currents! In 1992, a cargo ship in the Pacific Ocean accidentally dropped about twenty-nine thousand rubber ducks. Scientists studied where they washed up on land. The scientists used the data to create a resource map of ocean currents.

Glossary

agricultural: having to do with farming

average: a number that is calculated by adding quantities together and then dividing the total by the number of quantities

cartographer: a person who makes maps

census: a survey that counts the population of a country, city, or town

data: facts or information used to calculate, analyze, or plan something

hospitality: friendly treatment of visitors and guests

invasive species: plants or animals that are not native to an area and can cause harm to that area

key: an explanatory list of symbols on a map. Keys are also called legends.

percentage: the count or portion of a whole

quantity: the total count of something

ratio: the relationship in quantity, amount, or size between two or more things

scale: a tool that explains the size of a map compared to the actual place it represents

tourism: an economic activity related to travel

Learn More about Economic and Resource Maps

Books

Gillett, Jack, and Meg Gillett. *Natural Resource Maps.* New York: PowerKids, 2013. Learn more about natural resources, environmental issues, and maps that help illustrate these topics.

Higgins, Nadia. *US Geography through Infographics.* Minneapolis: Lerner Publications, 2015. Explore US geography by examining infographics, or pictures that share information.

Hirsch, Rebecca E. *Using Political Maps.* Minneapolis: Lerner Publications, 2017. Map lovers will enjoy learning about political maps of states, countries, and other places created by people.

Websites

Enchanted Learning: World Geography
http://www.enchantedlearning.com/geography
Check out this collection of maps, printouts, flags, and more from Enchanted Learning.

State Facts for Students
http://www.census.gov/schools/facts
At this Census Bureau site, you can look up all kinds of fun facts about your state, including how many nine-year-olds live there, how many toy stores it has, and whether the number of spots to buy candy in your state is growing or shrinking.

World Factbook: **Maps**
https://www.cia.gov/library/publications/the-world-factbook/docs/refmaps.html
This site is chock-full of regional and world maps of all kinds.

Index

Photo Acknowledgments

The images in this book are used with the permission of: © Lonely Planet Images/Getty Images, p. 4; © Laura Westlund/Independent Picture Service, pp. 5, 6, 7, 9, 13, 14, 15, 16, 20, 22, 23, 27, 28, 32, 35; © Pascalou95/Dreamstime.com, p. 8; © Roger Ressmeyer/Corbis, p. 10; © iStockphoto.com/blackwaterimages, p. 11; © Jackbluee/Dreamstime.com, p. 12; U.S. Census Bureau, pp. 17, 21; Institute of Museum and Library Services, p. 18; © Encyclopaedia Britannica/UIG/Getty Images, p. 19; Centers for Disease Control and Prevention, pp. 24, 26; © Illustrated London News Ltd/Mar/Pantheon/SuperStock, p. 25; © louise murray/Alamy, p. 29; COSMO-SkyMed Images– © ASI 2012, processed by e-geos, daily ice coverage information courtesy of US National Ice Centre, mapsheet created by Telespazio VEGA UK Ltd, p. 30; © Richard B. Levine/SuperStock, p. 31; © iStockphoto.com/NetaDegany, p. 33; © iStockphoto.com/Ken Brown, p. 34; © iStockphoto.com//iofoto, p. 36.

Front cover: © Laura Westlund/Independent Picture Service (map); © iStockphoto.com/Devaev Dmitriy (background).

Main body text set in Adrianna Regular 14/20.
Typeface provided by Chank.